The Reading Robot

By Judy Ling and Jill Carter

yes

Do you love me?
Let me guess.
Yes, no, **yes**, no,
yes, yes, yes!

"Moo," **went** the horse.
"Neigh," **went** the cow.
I think they are
muddled up . . . somehow.

3

am

I **am** five!
I **am** five!
And it's great
to be alive!

up

A cow and a goat
and a hairy baboon
went **up** to the moon
in a purple balloon.

walk

I can smile.
I can frown.
I can **walk** . . .
upside down.

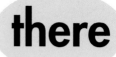

there

Who's **there**?
Who's **there**?
"Not me!"
growled the bear.

to

I swing low.
I swing high.
Down **to** the ground.
Up **to** the sky.

8

WHOO-ooo

"Where are you going?"
I asked the wind.
"Around the sky,"
was **his** reply.

likes

Johnny is disgusting.
Munch, munch, munch.
Johnny **likes** eating
slimy slugs for lunch.

10

I moo and chew—
that's what I do.
Who am I?
A cow . . . that's **who!**

here

Here are my eyes.
Here is my nose.
Here are my hands.
And **here** are my toes.

some

Put your frown away,
back where it belongs.
Get out your
happy smile
and sing **some**
happy songs!

13

under

We have a queen.
We live **under**
the ground.
We lay eggs
that are fat and round.

14

going

I'm **going** in my car.
I'm **going** fast and far.
Vroom, vroom, vroom!
I am **going** in my car.

15

into

Ice cream is yummy.
Ice cream is scrummy.
Ice cream goes **into**
the space in my tummy.

16